INVESTIGATING

DNA and BLOOD

INVESTIGATING

CRIME
SCENE
INVESTIGATORS

DNA and BLOOD

Ellina
Litmanovich
and
Sara L. Latta

Enslow Publishing
101 W. 23rd Street
Suite 240
New York, NY 10011
USA

enslow.com

Published in 2018 by Enslow Publishing, LLC.
101 W. 23rd Street, Suite 240, New York, NY 10011

Library of Congress Cataloging-in-Publication Data

Names: Litmanovich, Ellina, author. | Latta, Sara L., author.
Title: Investigating DNA and blood / Ellina Litmanovich and Sara L. Latta.
Description: New York, NY : Enslow Publishing, 2018. | Series: Crime scene
   investigators | Audience: Grades 5-8. | Includes bibliographical references
   and index.
Identifiers: LCCN 2017014012 | ISBN 9780766091849 (library bound) | ISBN
9780766095441 (paperback)
Subjects: LCSH: DNA fingerprinting—Juvenile literature. | DNA—Analysis—
   Juvenile literature.
Classification: LCC RA1057.55 .L58 2018 | DDC 614/.1—dc23
LC record available at https://lccn.loc.gov/2017014012

Printed in China

To Our Readers: We have done our best to make sure all website addresses in this book were active and appropriate when we went to press. However, the author and the publisher have no control over and assume no liability for the material available on those websites or on any websites they may link to. Any comments or suggestions can be sent by email to customerservice@ enslow.com.

Portions of this book appeared in the book *DNA and Blood: Dead People Do Tell Tales.*

Photo Credits: Cover and interior pages (blood stains, top and bottom) Zerbor/ Shutterstock.com; cover and interior pages (single blood stain) Sunflowerr/ Shutterstock.com; cover and interior pages (magnifying glass) azure1/ Shutterstock.com; cover and interior pages (genetic data background) kentoh/ Shutterstock.com; interior page backgrounds, p. 25 Nik Merkulov/Shutterstock .com; p. 6 ESB Professional/Shutterstock.com; pp. 8-9 Bliznetsov/E+/Getty Images; pp. 10, 50-51 © AP Images; pp. 14, 78 Bettmann/Getty Images; p. 16 KRT/Newscom; p. 18 Couperfield/Shutterstock.com; p. 21 Jim Varney/ Science Source; p. 29 FBI/Science Source; p. 31 ullstein bild/Getty Images; p. 35 Barbol/Shutterstock.com; pp. 36-37 Stastny_Pavel/Shutterstock.com; pp. 40-41 lkordela/Shutterstock.com; p. 47 Designua/Shutterstock.com; p. 54 Knorre/Shutterstock.com; p. 56 Kim Kulish/AFP/Getty Images; pp. 60-61 Don Tormey/Los Angeles Times/Getty Images; pp. 64-65 Creativa Images/ Shutterstock.com; pp. 66-67 Christian Science Monitor/Getty Images; p. 70 Library of Congress Prints and Photographs Division; p. 72 SVF2/Universal Images Group/Getty Images; p. 75 NoPainNoGain/Shutterstock.com; pp. 82-83 Wolfgang Kaehler/LightRocket/Getty Images; pp. 84-85 Joe Amon/Denver Post/Getty Images; p. 88 Carl De Souza/AFP/Getty Images; pp. 90-91 Georges Gobet/AFP/Getty Images.

CONTENTS

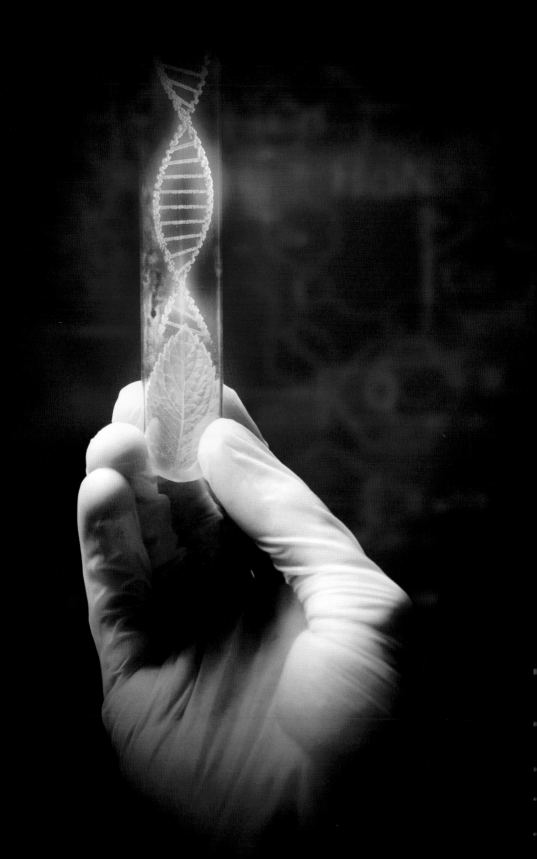

THE ANSWER IS IN DNA

Forensic science uses scientific principles in biology, physics, and chemistry to analyze evidence from crimes scenes. The findings are then presented in court to help prove a defendant's guilt or innocence. Some of the most important questions forensic science answers are: Who is the victim? How did he or she die? How long ago did the death occur? Did the perpetrator leave any evidence behind that could lead to his or her identity? New technology, specialized training, and advanced knowledge of how the body works and what happens to it after death have helped crime scene investigators close cases, some decades or even more than a century old, that would otherwise have been left unsolved.

Crime scene investigators look for evidence on and around a body to try to determine the circumstances surrounding the death.

One of the most crucial pieces of evidence an investigator could come upon is DNA (deoxyribonucleic acid), a molecule that carries a set of instructions and is found in the nucleus of every cell in an organism's body. Each person's DNA is unique to them, with the exception of identical twins. Each stretch of DNA is called a gene, which determines an individual's height, eye color, hair color, skin color, and all other physical traits.

When a forensic scientist examines the body of a murder victim, they look for blood-stains, fallen hairs, skin cells, saliva, as well as any other type of biological evidence that may have been left behind. They analyze the DNA in these items to create a DNA profile, or DNA fingerprint, of an individual in order to identify the victim, if unknown, and the criminal.

On December 6, 2005, Steven Avery appeared in court for his preliminary hearing for the murder of Teresa Halbach. The prosecutors had charred bone fragments, blood, and DNA as evidence against Avery.

The interest in crime scene investigation among the masses continues to grow as evidenced by the many fictional shows and true crime documentaries on television, such as *CSI, NCIS, Cold Case, Forensic Files, Snapped,* and *The Jinx.*

In 2016, the first season of the Netflix show, *Making a Murderer,* helped Steven Avery, a Wisconsin man, shoot to fame. In 2007, Avery, along with his nephew Brendan Dassey, was charged and sentenced to life in prison for the murder of Teresa Halbach, a twenty-five-year-old photographer who had been killed two years earlier. The documentary explored accusations that county officials tampered with blood evidence to frame Avery and Dassey for that murder. In 1985, Avery had been wrongfully convicted of sexual assault and attempted murder. After eighteen years in prison, he was exonerated with the help of the Innocence Project, an organization of attorneys and law students that use DNA technology to prove the innocence of people wrongfully convicted of serious crimes.

It is clearly evident that DNA plays a decisive role in a crime scene investigation. When properly handled, it can bring justice to victims—and innocent people who are wrongfully imprisoned.

CHAPTER 1

EVIDENCE OF BLOOD

As citizens of the United States, individuals have the right to be presumed innocent until proven guilty. Although a person can be charged with a crime, the court would need proof beyond a reasonable doubt—sufficient evidence and convincing—before the judge and jury could sentence and imprison the defendant. But even then, there is the possibility that the case was mishandled, which would then lead to a retrial and re-examination of the evidence.

Was It a False Accusation?

Sam Sheppard and his wife, Marilyn, lived in Cleveland, Ohio. Sheppard was a doctor at nearby Bay View Hospital. Dr. and Mrs. Sheppard had some friends over for dinner on the night of July 3, 1954. It had been a busy day for Dr. Sheppard. He had performed a scheduled surgery in the morning and an emergency surgery that afternoon, in an unsuccessful attempt to save the life of a young boy. He was called back to the hospital as he and his guests were having predinner cocktails, this time to tend to a boy with a broken leg. The guests left around midnight and Dr. Sheppard, exhausted from the day's events, fell asleep on the daybed in the living room. Mrs. Sheppard went upstairs to their bedroom.

Just before dawn, Spencer Houk's phone rang. "For God's sake, Spen, get over here!" Houk recognized the voice of his friend and neighbor, Sam Sheppard. "I think they've killed Marilyn."[1] Houk, who also happened to be the mayor of Bay Village, and his wife, Esther, arrived at the Sheppard home a few minutes later. Mrs. Houk found Mrs. Sheppard's bloody body upstairs.

The police were soon on the scene. They questioned Dr. Sheppard briefly, and he told them that he had been awakened by his wife's cries. He headed upstairs to the bedroom, where he caught a glimpse of a figure before being hit on the back of the neck. When he came to, he found his wife lying in a pool of blood on the bed, and the bedroom was flecked with red spatters. He checked for her pulse. There was none. His seven-year-old son, Samuel Reese (nicknamed Chip), slept soundly in his bedroom.

According to Dr. Sheppard, he had heard a noise below and ran down the stairs just in time to see someone running toward the lake behind his home. He chased the man, later described as being 6 feet 3

On July 22, 1954, Dr. Samuel Sheppard revealed what he could recall about the death of his wife, Marilyn, on the witness stand. He wore a neck brace due to injuries he said he received during a struggle with his wife's murderer.

inches (190.5 centimeters) tall and middle-aged with bushy hair. He reached the man but was knocked out again. When he awoke, the intruder was gone—this time for good. Dr. Sheppard claimed to have suffered a neck injury in the scuffle, and he clearly had bruises and cuts on his face.

Satisfied, the police allowed Dr. Sheppard's brother to take him to Bay View Hospital to treat his injuries. Chip was sent to the house of another uncle. The crime scene investigators were lax when it came to gathering fingerprints, and they allowed reporters into the house. Although they photographed the bedroom and footprints they found outside, they regarded the crime scene as little more than a bloody mess.

The police and coroner found that Mrs. Sheppard had thirty-five wounds, including fifteen blows to the head, and cuts on her hands, arms, and fingers.

The police were inclined to think that Dr. Sheppard had murdered his wife. It was a reasonable suspicion. At least 30 percent of women who are murdered are killed by people they know—usually a husband or boyfriend.[2] At the time, most of Cleveland thought that the wealthy, good-looking doctor was guilty of his wife's murder. Three weeks after the murder, Dr. Sheppard was arrested and charged with the crime.

The trial began on October 18, 1954. His defense attorney, William Corrigan, asked for a change of venue. The intense and biased media coverage

This 1954 crime scene photo of Marilyn Sheppard's murder shows a large blood stain on the carpet (*bottom left*).

would make it impossible for his client to get a fair hearing, he said. The request was denied.

At the trial, the prosecuting attorney said that Dr. Sheppard's story was too far-fetched. Most incriminating of all was the testimony of the medical technician, Susan Hayes, who said that she and Dr. Sheppard had been having an affair for three years. After six weeks of testimony, the jury found Dr. Sheppard guilty of second-degree murder. He was sentenced to life in prison.

Corrigan had made a big mistake. He didn't have his own experts examine the house along with the investigators. Corrigan called in a nationally known expert on forensic science and bloodstain pattern analysis to correct the mistake. The expert, Paul Kirk, agreed to take on the assignment but warned that he might only find further evidence of Dr. Sheppard's guilt.

Kirk measured and analyzed the shapes of blood drops in the Sheppards' bedroom. The walls were spattered with blood, except in one corner of the room. Something had blocked the flying drops of blood; probably the killer's own body. Dr. Sheppard would have been covered with blood, but other than a small bloodstain on his pants, there was no blood on him. Kirk also noticed an unusual bloodstain on the closet door that was much larger than the other spatters. He could tell from the large size of the stain that it would have traveled only inches before hitting the door. It couldn't have come from the bed

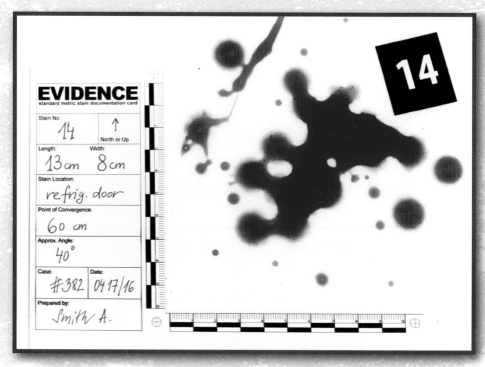

EVIDENCE
standard metric stain documentation card

Stain No.	
14	↑ North or Up

Length:	Width:
13 cm	8 cm

Stain Location:
refrig. door

Point of Convergence:
60 cm

Approx. Angle:
40°

Case:	Date:
#382	04 17/16

Prepared by:
Smith A.

Bloodstain pattern analysts carefully record details about blood stains found at crime scenes, including each stain's measurements, shape, and location.

where Mrs. Sheppard had been lying. Kirk deduced that Mrs. Sheppard, in a desperate struggle for her life, had wounded the killer.

The police found two of Mrs. Sheppard's teeth on the bed underneath her body. Kirk did some experiments with teeth he acquired from dentists. He determined that Mrs. Sheppard's teeth had been pulled from the inside out. Kirk proposed that Mrs. Sheppard had sunk her teeth into the killer's hand as he tried to cover her mouth to stifle her cries. At the time, there were no bite marks or other injuries on Dr. Sheppard's hands.

The theory of a wounded killer also explained the blood trail leading out of the bedroom, down the stairs, and out of the house. The prosecution claimed that Dr. Sheppard had carried the weapon through the house, dripping blood as he went. But Kirk showed that it was impossible for a murder weapon to retain enough blood to have created such a long trail—forty drops of blood. The blood must have come from the injured killer, he said.

Kirk also carried out blood-typing tests on the blood spots. He knew that Mrs. Sheppard had type O blood; Dr. Sheppard's was type A. But the results were inconclusive, in part, because it was difficult to use the technology available at the time to determine blood type in such old samples.

Kirk wrote up his findings in a report with this conclusion: "Taken together, the only explanation that actually is consistent with all the facts is the one given by Sam, vague and uncertain though it may be."[3] Corrigan submitted the report and asked for a new trial based on this new evidence. His request was denied.

Sam Sheppard spent the next ten years in prison, even as Corrigan continued to try to get a new trial. When Corrigan died in 1961, the Sheppard family hired a rising young lawyer named F. Lee Bailey to take on Dr. Sheppard's case. Bailey argued before the US Supreme Court that his client had not been

Analyzing Blood

Bloodstains, or blood spatter, can provide valuable clues about how—or whether—a crime was committed. When a drop of blood hits a surface, it leaves a stain with a distinctive shape. Passive bloodstains are created when blood drips to a surface from gravity alone.

Transfer stains occur when wet blood on one surface comes into contact with another surface. Projected stains, or trajectory, are made when blood is propelled to a surface under a force greater than gravity alone.

Bloodstain pattern analysis experts spend hours documenting and measuring the size and shape of bloodstains. They may attach strings to each individual blood spatter to see where they come together, or converge. They also use computer programs to create three-dimensional models and animations that show how and where the bloodstains were made. This is useful for blood pattern analysis experts who are presenting evidence to a jury.

A bloodstain pattern analyst simulates an assault on a victim by dropping a piece of wood on a bloody pig carcass. The impact produces droplets of blood that land in a distinct pattern. This information helps investigators figure out the details of a crime.

given a fair trial. The court agreed, and in 1966 Dr. Sheppard was granted a second trial.

The Retrial

When the time for a retrial arrived, F. Lee Bailey used Kirk as the star witness for the defense. The blood evidence was enough to convince the jury, who returned the verdict of not guilty.

Sam Sheppard was a free man physically, but not mentally. Many people still believed he was guilty. He turned to alcohol and drugs, and he died of liver failure just four years later.

After his father's death, Samuel Reese Sheppard spent years trying to clear his father's name. In 1999, Mr. Sheppard sued the state of Ohio for the wrongful imprisonment of his father. He had DNA tests carried out on old samples of his parents' blood as well as on a sample of blood from the man he believed had committed the crime, Richard Eberling. However, the samples had been collected decades before DNA testing was developed and long before scientists knew how to preserve blood evidence without contamination. The test results were not conclusive. In 2000, after a ten-week trial, a civil jury declared that Sheppard failed to prove that his father had been wrongfully imprisoned.

The Sheppard case marked an important milestone in acknowledging the role of bloodstain evidence in the legal system. Mrs. Sheppard's killer has never been found.

CHAPTER 2

BLOOD OR DYE?

o the naked eye, there are many things that may resemble blood: paint, food stains, dyes. Prior to the use of chemical tests, there were few ways of finding out if something was a human bloodstain or another substance. For centuries, criminals were able to get away with murder because no one could prove that dried bloodstains were, in fact, blood.

The Carpenter

In 1898, in the German village of Lechtingen, Hannelore Heidemann and Else Langemeier didn't return from school. The girls' worried mothers visited the school, learning that the friends had not been to class that day. The villagers searched the nearby woods for evidence of the girls. As daylight was fading, someone found Hannelore's body lying among some trees. Some time later, Else's remains were also found.

A man wearing an apron that appeared to be stained with dark liquid had been seen entering the village from the woods. His name was Ludwig Tessnow. Upon questioning, Tessnow explained that he was a carpenter, and the stains were wood dye. To test his claim, a policeman visited Tessnow in his workshop and "accidentally" knocked over a tin of wood dye onto Tessnow's pants. It looked exactly like the stains on the carpenter's apron. They concluded that he was telling the truth. Someone more experienced would have used a microscope to see the telltale signs of red blood cells.

As attacks happened often in the winter when prey was scarce, the villagers persuaded themselves that the girls had been the victims of a hungry wolf. Perhaps it was easier for the villagers to believe this over the alternative.

Early the following year, Tessnow left Lechtingen.

The Carpenter Strikes Again

Two and a half years later, strange things began to happen near Göhren, a village on an island off the northern coast of Germany. A farmer found the mutilated bodies of seven of his sheep. He had seen a man running away from his farm. The farmer swore that if he saw the man again, he would be able to recognize him.

Three weeks later, Hermann and Peter Stubbe left home to play. They never came back. Their bodies were found the following morning with their

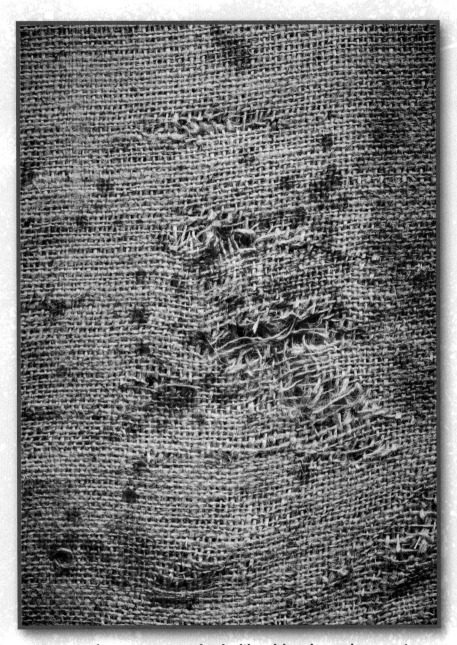

Many substances can look like blood, such as wine stains (pictured here) and wood dye. Chemical tests or a microscope would be needed to confirm it is blood.

skulls crushed by a rock. A villager remembered that he had seen the two boys talking to the odd carpenter Tessnow the day they had disappeared. The police searched Tessnow's home and found clothing and boots with dark stains, all recently washed. It was all part of the trade and caused by wood dye, Tessnow insisted.

The village judge recalled the killings in Lechtingen several years earlier and contacted the police there. Their main suspect, a carpenter named Ludwig Tessnow, swore that the stains had been caused by wood dye. Meanwhile, the farmer whose sheep had been hacked to pieces had no trouble picking Tessnow out of a lineup.

The judge, Johann-Klaus Schmidt, was sure that Tessnow was their man. But how could they prove it? Schmidt's friend, a prosecutor named Ernst Hubschmann, recalled reading a report about a new scientific test for human bloodstains. The test could detect bloodstains even on clothing that had been washed, and it could distinguish between human and animal blood.

Tessnow's stained clothing and the bloodstained rock that was believed to be the murder weapon were sent to Paul Uhlenhuth, the author of the new scientific article. Uhlenhuth and his assistant examined each and every stain on the clothing. They dissolved the stains in water and salt solutions, testing them for hemoglobin, an iron-containing protein in blood that carries oxygen throughout the body. Many of the stains were wood dye, but twenty-six were definitely bloodstains.

By using his new human-protein test, Uhlenhuth was able to prove that the bloodstains were from human blood. Never again would a murderer get away with the claim that the blood of his victims was something other than blood or that it was the blood of an animal. Ludwig Tessnow was found guilty of the murders and put to death three years later.

Is It Human or Animal Blood?

In 1885, Louis Pasteur saved the life of a boy who had been bitten by a rabid dog by injecting him with a weakened version of the deadly rabies virus. This was the birth of a new science called immunology.

In 1900, scientist Paul Uhlenhuth from Vienna, Austria, carried out a series of experiments in which he injected chicken blood into rabbits. When he added a drop of chicken blood to a test tube of serum from the inoculated rabbits, the liquid turned cloudy. But when blood from cows, pigs, sheep, or horses was added to serum from the inoculated animal, the mixture remained clear. The rabbits had not formed antibodies against cow, pig, sheep, or horse antigens, because they had only been injected with chicken blood. Uhlenhuth concluded that the blood of different animals had characteristic proteins not shared by the blood of other animals.

He showed that a rabbit injected with human blood—even dried blood—would produce a serum

Identifying Blood

f you find someone lying in a pool of red liquid flowing from a hole in his chest, there's a good chance that the liquid is blood. But what if you found a crumpled T-shirt with rust-colored stains stashed behind the bushes near a murder scene? Without a proper test for blood, it would be difficult to determine whether the owner is guilty of murder.

As early as 1853, a German scientist found that by adding acid and salt to a drop of blood, then heating the mixture, crystals would form. This test depends on the presence of hemoglobin in red blood cells.

Today, forensic scientists have additional reliable presumptive tests for blood. One, called the Kastle-Meyer test, uses a chemical indicator, phenolphthalein, and hydrogen peroxide. The hydrogen peroxide reacts with hemoglobin to create water plus a highly reactive form of oxygen. This form of oxygen reacts with the indicator molecule, changing it from colorless to bright pink.

Modern forensic scientists may also test the stain or scene of a crime with luminol, a chemical that gives off a faint bluish glow when it reacts with hemoglobin and hydrogen peroxide. It is so

Luminol makes bloodstains glow. Forensic investigators use it to find trace amounts of blood, which may not be visible to the naked eye, present at a crime scene.

sensitive that it can detect blood on clothing that have been machine-washed. Even if the murderer scrubs down the crime scene, it is nearly impossible to get rid of every trace of blood. Luminol can often detect it.

These tests only suggest the presence of blood. There can be false positives, so they must be used carefully in a court of law. But they may be a very useful first step in investigating a crime scene.

that reacted specifically with human blood. He immediately recognized just how important this test would be to forensic science. "Judges and experts have for a long time been most deeply concerned with the all-important problem of distinguishing human blood from other blood types," he wrote. "Until now, though, a sure answer to this question has been impossible [in the case of dried blood]. . . . Since in forensic practice one is almost exclusively concerned with such dried blood, one must be equipped with a practical, forensic method to determine also the origins of blood in this condition."[1]

Today, forensic scientists have a fast, easy-to-use version of Uhlenhuth's precipitin test to determine what species a blood sample came from. The test is so sensitive that it can detect tiny amounts of blood in a stain that is decades old.

The Holmes Test

Arthur Conan Doyle introduced Sherlock Holmes to the world in 1887, with the publication of A Study in Scarlet. The detective had just discovered an infallible test for bloodstains:

> "I've found it! I've found it," he shouted to my companion, running towards us with a test-tube in his hand. "I have found a re-agent which is precipitated by haemoglobin, and by nothing else. . . . Criminal cases are continually hinging upon that one point. A man is suspected of a crime months perhaps after it has been committed. His linen or clothes are examined and brownish stains discovered upon them. Are

An illustration from the first edition of *A Study in Scarlet* shows (*left to right*) Inspector Lestrade, Sherlock Holmes, Dr. Watson, and Inspector Gregson.

they bloodstains, or mud stains, or rust stains, or fruit stains, or what are they? That is a question which has puzzled many an expert, and why? Because there was no reliable test. Now we have the Sherlock Holmes's test, and there will no longer be any difficulty."[2]

When *A Study in Scarlet* was first published, people thought that the Holmes test was fictional. In 1987, chemist Christine L. Huber showed that the Holmes test was no mere storytelling device. Using chemicals that would have been available to Conan Doyle, Huber followed the procedure described in the story—and got the same results. "How [the test] was lost in the first place and why Holmes never received acknowledgement for it remains a mystery," Huber wrote. "Perhaps it is enough, however, to know that in his centennial year Sherlock Holmes has been vindicated as the wisest and best chemist whom it has been our pleasure to know."[3]

FORENSIC SEROLOGY

erology is the testing of blood serum to find antibodies in the blood. In 1909 Viennese scientist Karl Landsteiner discovered that human red blood cells carry certain sugar molecules, or antigens, that can vary from one person to another. Some people carry the A antigen on their red blood cells (type A), some carry the B antigen (type B), and some carry both (type AB). Some people carry neither the A nor the B antigen (type O).

In the 1920s, a Japanese scientist named Saburo Sirai discovered that 80 percent of the population had these same blood group antigens in other bodily fluids. For these people, called secretors, investigators can determine blood type by testing body fluids, such as saliva, tears, or urine.

The following two cases illustrate how the discoveries of these two scientists helped authorities identify the suspects involved.

Bloody Washcloths and Hairs

Eight-year-old Helen Priestly was well liked by everyone in the neighborhood where she lived with her parents in Aberdeen, Scotland. Everyone, it seems, except Jeannie Donald. Her daughter had once been Helen's friend, but the girls had quarreled. Jeannie would scowl at Helen as she passed on the street and scold her when she played nearby. Helen, in turn, liked to taunt her neighbor with the nickname "Coconut," in reference to the woman's frizzy hair.

Early in the afternoon of April 20, 1934, Helen's mother sent her out to buy some bread at a nearby shop. When she failed to return, her mother went out to look for her. Yes, said the shop staff, they had seen Helen. She had bought her loaf of bread around 1:30 p.m. Someone had seen her walking home around 1:45 p.m.

Within a few hours, the police and hundreds of local people turned out to look for Helen. Her body was found strangled, sexually assaulted, and stuffed in a large, blue sack in the apartment building's common bathroom on the ground floor. The police questioned everyone in the building. Jeannie Donald had an alibi, but details of her story didn't pan out. The police searched the Donalds' apartment and found what appeared to be bloodstains. The Donalds were soon behind bars. Mr. Donald's alibi held up, so he was released. Police attention rested solely upon Jeannie Donald.

They called in Sydney Smith, professor of forensic medicine at Edinburgh University, to help investigate. He turned his attention first to the blue sack in which Helen's body had been found. He found fibers as well as cat, rabbit, and human hair. Some of the human hair matched Helen's, but some hairs were distinctly different. He examined all of them under a microscope, comparing them with samples taken from the Donald household and other apartments in the building. He found twenty-five fibers in the

An image of a human hair under a microscope reveals its structure. Hairs found at crime scenes can be matched to victims and suspects.

Donald home that matched fibers from the blue sack. None of the other apartments had matching fibers.

Next, he turned his attention to some evidence that the police had missed. He found bloodstains on two washcloths, a cleaning brush, a package of soap, the floor, and a newspaper dated the day before the murder. His laboratory found the blood to be type O, the same as Helen Priestly's blood. Jeannie had type A blood. So far, everything seemed to point to Jeannie's guilt. But about half of the world's population has type O blood, so it would be impossible to prove that the blood was Helen's.

Then Smith had a brilliant idea. He knew that Helen's intestine had been split open during that attack. Knowing that we all carry billions of bacteria in our intestines, he guessed that some of the bacteria might have been released into Helen's blood. Smith sent some

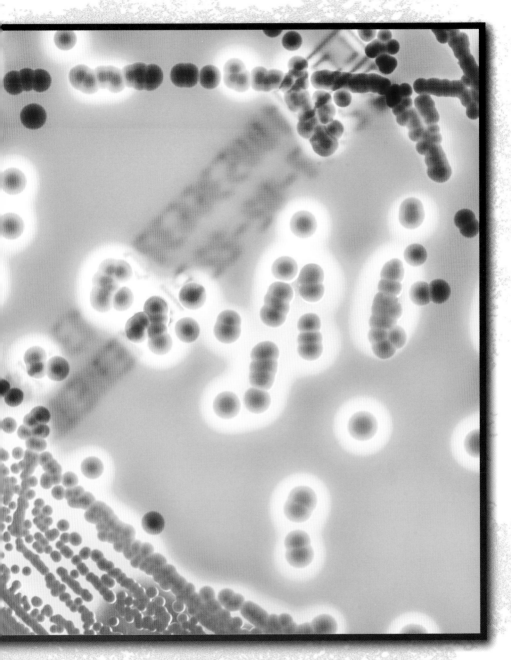

This is a close-up of *Streptococcus* bacteria, of which several species can be found in a person's mouth, skin, intestine, and upper respiratory tract. Each individual's microbiome is unique.

Fingerprinting Through Bacteria

Sydney Smith was way ahead of his time in recognizing that individuals could be identified by the unique bacteria that live in their bodies. The typical human body is home to a huge number of microbes. In fact, there are ten times more microbial cells in your body than human cells. They live in our mouths, in our intestines, and on our skin. Each of us carries with us a set of bacteria that is unique to us, in terms of the numbers and types of species and strains.

"Each one of us leaves a unique trail of bugs behind us as we travel through our daily lives," said Noah Fierer, an assistant professor at the University of Colorado at Boulder. Fierer and his colleagues took samples of bacteria deposited on the personal keyboards of different computer users. Using gene-sequencing techniques, they created a DNA profile of all the bacteria deposited on those surfaces. The bacterial DNA taken from the keys of the computer owners matched that of the owners much more closely than that of samples taken from random keyboards and fingertips.

"While this project is still in its preliminary stages, we think the technique could eventually become a valuable new item in the toolbox of forensic scientists," Fierer said.[1]

of Helen's bloodstained clothing and bloodstained articles from the Donald apartment to a professor of bacteriology at Edinburgh University. The bacteriologist found considerable amounts of bacteria in Helen's bloodstained clothing and on the washcloths. But the clincher was that both Helen's blood and the washcloths contained a highly unusual strain of bacteria.

Smith proposed that Jeannie had had enough of Helen's taunting and had killed her in a fit of rage. He concluded that the washcloths had been used to mop up Helen's blood. The jury believed him, and Jeannie Donald was sentenced to life in prison.

Saliva on Cigarette Butts

The Priestly-Donald case was the first one in which blood-typing played an important role in solving the case. In 1939, the young science of forensic serology seemed to take two steps forward and one step back in a famous case involving a murder, a glass, and cigarette butts.

On May 21, 1939, a businessman named Walter Dinivan was badly beaten in his apartment on the southern coast of England. He died later that night. Chief Inspector Leonard Burt of Scotland Yard examined the crime scene carefully. All the evidence pointed to robbery. Dinivan's living room safe had been opened with his keys and emptied of its contents. A crumpled paper bag lay on the floor, and two glasses were resting on the table in the sitting room, suggesting Dinivan had been having a drink with someone. There were also a number of cigarette butts scattered about.

Inspector Burt examined the apartment for fingerprints, including the glasses. He found fingerprints that matched Dinivan and members of his family. But there was a print on one of the glasses that didn't match any of the others. On the chance that the murderer was a secretor—a person whose blood antigens can also be found in his saliva—Inspector Burt had his lab test the cigarette butts. The lab results came back: the saliva residue on the cigarettes showed that whoever had smoked them had type AB blood. This is generally the rarest type of blood. It is found in just 3 percent of the Caucasian population.

While interviewing Dinivan's family and acquaintances, the name Joseph Williams came up. Williams had been a friend of Dinivan's. Unlike Dinivan, he was chronically broke, although he had come into a large sum of money around May 21. When questioned by the police, he admitted that he had been angry with Dinivan, who had refused to loan him some money. But he said that he won the money betting on a horse race. He refused to let the police get a sample of his fingerprints or to submit to a blood test.

Inspector Burt was clever. He ordered his officers to keep an eye on Williams and to let him know if his suspect entered a pub. A few days later the

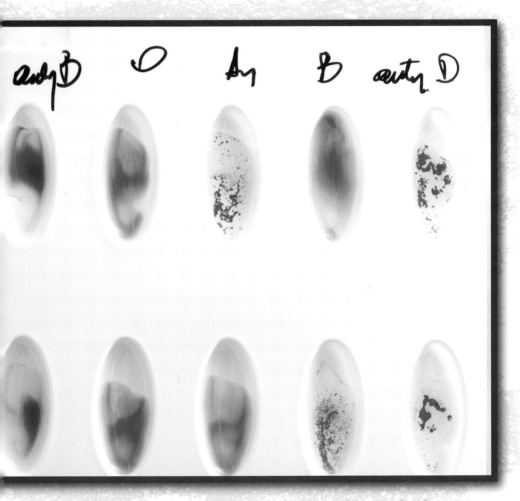

To determine blood type, a scientist adds antibodies to blood samples and observes how they react. For example, anti-A antibodies will cause type A and type AB blood cells to clump together, but not type B or type O blood cells.

USING BLOOD TO PREDICT AGE

In March 2017, researchers at King's College in London discovered a new forensic technique that could predict the age of suspects from blood and saliva collected at crime scenes by employing machine learning. Machine learning is a type of artificial intelligence in which the computer is not specifically programmed but uses algorithms to learn from data.

Using sixteen biomarkers in blood samples, the researchers were able to correctly predict the ages of sample donors within an average of four years. This new method could provide forensic investigators with leads on difficult cases and narrow their suspect pool.[2]

inspector rushed to a pub where he "accidentally" ran into Williams. Burt offered him a drink and a cigarette, both of which Williams accepted. They chatted about horse racing for the next hour or so, and Burt kept Williams busy with a steady supply of alcohol and cigarettes. After Williams staggered out of the bar, Burt carefully gathered the contents of the ashtray and had them sent to his lab to be tested for blood type.

Williams was a secretor. His blood type was AB.

Armed with this information, Burt searched Williams's apartment. He found a bundle of paper bags exactly like the one that had been found in Dinivan's apartment—which Burt suspected had been wrapped around the murder weapon. Williams insisted he was innocent, daring Burt to take his fingerprints. Burt did so, and found a match to the mystery print on the glass in Dinivan's apartment.

The money, the fingerprint, the rare blood type—the evidence against Williams seemed to be strong, even though there was no direct evidence to place him with Dinivan on the night of the murder. At the trial, Williams's lawyer held up one of the cigarette butts. How was it possible, he asked them, to determine a blood type from traces of saliva on a cigarette butt?

The jury found Williams not guilty. That night, after an evening of drinking, Williams confessed to a reporter, "I've got to tell somebody. You see the jury was wrong . . . it was me."[3]

Clearly, serology can be a useful tool in forensic science—but only to a point. In some cases, blood-typing is more useful for excluding a particular suspect than for including another. Here's why: say investigators test a bloody knife found at the scene of a stabbing murder. They find that on the knife there is a mixture of type AB blood, matching that of the victim, and type A blood from another individual. One suspect turns out to have type O blood, so clearly it was not his blood on the knife. Another suspect does have type A blood—but so do approximately 45 percent of all Caucasians! And this is where a technique called DNA fingerprinting becomes critical.

DNA PROFILING

n 1984, British geneticist Alec Jeffreys developed a new technique called DNA fingerprinting, also known as DNA profiling. In recent years, DNA profiles have been used to identify the origins of DNA samples found at crime scenes. When a criminal commits a crime, not only are his or her fingerprints added to a national database, but samples of his or her DNA are entered as well. If that same criminal commits another crime, his or her prints and DNA are already in the system, and he or she may be caught quickly.

Applying PCR Technology to STRs in DNA

Most people have twenty-three pairs of chromosomes packed into the nucleus of nearly every cell in their bodies. One set of chromosomes comes from the mother's egg; the other comes from the father's sperm. Each chromosome contains a strand of tightly coiled DNA, which would resemble a twisted ladder with rungs if you were to stretch it out. The rungs of the ladder are made of three billion bonded pairs of subunits called nucleotides. There are four different types of nucleotide bases in DNA: adenine (A), thymine (T), cytosine (C), and guanine (G). Adenine always bonds with thymine, and cytosine always bonds with guanine. The nucleotides are arranged into genes. Because we inherit one gene from each parent, we have two copies, or alleles, of each gene.

The majority of human DNA is the same for all humans. Most of us share basic characteristics, after all: one head, two arms, two legs, 206 bones. But there are stretches of DNA, or loci, that do not appear to have any function—or, at any rate, do not code for any genes. These loci, called short tandem repeats (STRs), contain short segments of DNA that are repeated one after another in different numbers from one individual to another. Since these loci do not code for any genes, they can vary dramatically without affecting the health of an individual. STRs are used in DNA profiling. The technique was first used to solve a criminal case in 1987, when police in the United Kingdom collected blood samples from more than five thousand people in order to identify the man who had murdered two young women.

DNA structure

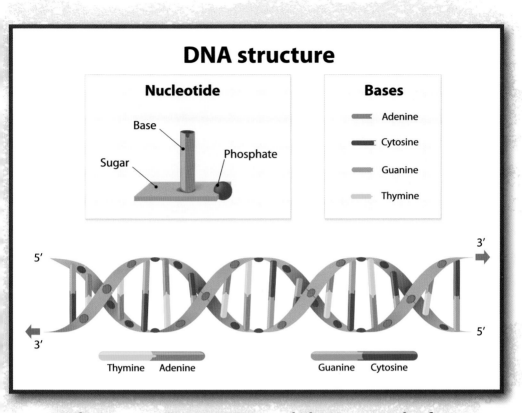

Nucleotide

Base

Sugar

Phosphate

Bases

Adenine

Cytosine

Guanine

Thymine

5'

3'

3'

5'

Thymine Adenine

Guanine Cytosine

Adenine, cytosine, guanine, and thymine are the four types of nucleotide bases found in DNA. How they are arranged determines a person's genetic traits.

Let's say that crime scene investigators find skin cells under the fingernails of a woman who was murdered. They suspect that the skin came from the murderer, scratched off as the woman tried to defend herself. The investigators may wear masks, disposable coveralls, booties, and gloves when collecting evidence. Evidence must not become contaminated with DNA from the investigators or other people.

In the laboratory, scientists break up the skin cells and extract and purify the DNA. They copy the DNA and the thirteen STR regions that vary from person to person, using a polymerase chain reaction, or PCR, technology. Sometimes described as "molecular photocopying," PCR amplifies even minute amounts of DNA until there is enough material for analysis.[1] This is especially useful if the sample is very small or old.

By determining the type of the sample's STR loci, forensic scientists create a DNA profile for the individual. Although there are more than two thousand STR loci that could be tested, only a few of them are routinely used for forensic DNA profiling. In the United States, the FBI (Federal Bureau of Investigation) uses thirteen markers. The likelihood that two people (with the exception of identical twins) will have the same DNA profile at all thirteen loci is one in 10 billion—or greater. Specific DNA profiles are stored in a computer database called the Combined DNA Index System (CODIS). Forensic laboratories all across the country have access to this database.

Armed with a DNA profile of the suspect, the forensic scientist searches for a match using CODIS. He strikes gold—the profile matches that of the woman's ex-boyfriend, who had been in the CODIS database after being convicted for an earlier crime.

The Xbox Killers

Erin Belanger and her boyfriend, Francisco "Flaco" Ayo-Roman, moved from Massachusetts to Deltona, Florida, in 2004. Twenty-two-year-old Belanger and thirty-year-old Ayo-Roman shared a house on Telford Lane with their friends Michelle Ann Nathan and Anthony Vega and a pet dachshund named George. Other friends, Robert "Tito" Gonzalez and Jonathan Gleason, sometimes stayed with them.

Belanger and Ayo-Roman had been living in Deltona only four months when Belanger discovered that someone was illegally living in her grandmother's winter home across town. The man, Troy Victorino, had left papers and credit card receipts bearing his name scattered around the place. Furious, Belanger gathered up his belongings—clothes, drugs, CDs, and an Xbox game system—and took them to her house. She called the police.

It was too risky for Victorino, a man with a criminal record and a reputation for violence, to go to the house to get his belongings. He asked his friends to go instead. He waited in the shadows while three of his friends rang the doorbell. An argument broke out, and Belanger dialed 911. "I don't want problems," she told the operator. "Oh, my God. All I did was want to get people that were living in my nana's house out."[2]

After hearing that the police were on their way, Victorino and his friends fled—but not before slashing the tires of two vehicles in the driveway. "I want them dead," he said.[3]

Three days later, Victorino and his friends were seen shopping for aluminum bats at Walmart. A store clerk asked one of the men if they needed any help. No, the man said. "He had a nasty attitude," the clerk later said.[4] Another store employee recalled the men joking about using the bats to bash people's heads in.

Early in the morning of August 6, 2004, Christopher Carroll came by the house on Telford Lane. A friend from Burger King had sent him there to check up on Gonzalez, who hadn't shown up for work that morning. The door had been kicked in, and from the entrance of the doorway, he could see three bodies. The house was in shambles and blood was everywhere.

The police arrived to find the four men, two women, and the little dog who had been living at Telford Lane dead. Investigators believed from the outset that the killer—or killers—had known the victims. Troy Victorino immediately came to mind.

Two days later, police arrested Troy Victorino, Robert Cannon, Jerone Hunter, and Michael Salas for the six murders. Cannon, Hunter, and Salas all confessed to the crimes, but Victorino steadfastly maintained his innocence. All three men were found guilty of first-degree murder and other charges. The strongest testimony against Victorino at the trial came from Florida Department of Law Enforcement

During the murder trial against the "Xbox killers," Stacy Colton, a crime scene investigator, points to the areas in the home where the six bodies were found.

DNA expert Emily Booth Varan. She found blood on a pair of boots prosecutors believed Victorino had worn on the night of the killings. The stains contained "a DNA profile that matched Erin Belanger's standard," Varan said, adding that it would take 750,000 times the world population of six billion to find a similar match.[5] She also found a bloodstain on the heel of the left boot that matched the DNA profile of Vega, and a third that corresponded to that of Ayo-Roman. Most of the DNA from sweat and skin cells Varan recovered from inside the boot matched Victorino's profile. Bloody footprints matching the boots were found at the crime scene. Varan also found blood from Nathan, Gonzalez, and Vega on Hunter's sneakers.

The DNA evidence sealed the case. Troy Victorino and Jerone Hunter were sentenced to death by lethal injection. Robert Cannon and Michael Salas are serving life sentences.

The massacre, which would become known nationwide as the "Xbox murders," was about more than simple revenge over a missing gaming system. A conversation Victorino had with a fellow inmate while awaiting trial points to a deeper motivation: hunger for respect. "He claims he is a Latin King," said the inmate. "He is this big gang leader and they basically disrespected him and he had to deal with that because they couldn't treat a King like that."[6]

Katie's Law

Katie Sepich, a graduate student at New Mexico State University, was murdered in 2003. There were no strong suspects, but investigators used skin and blood under her fingernails to create a DNA profile of her attacker. They entered the DNA profile into CODIS, but there were no matches.

Sepich's parents learned that most states allow law enforcement officials to take DNA only from people who have been convicted of a felony—not from those simply arrested for one. Just three months after Sepich's murder, a man named Gabriel Avilla was arrested but not convicted, on a felony charge. When Avilla was convicted of another felony crime in 2006, his DNA profile was entered into CODIS. It matched that of Sepich's killer. Had the DNA sample been taken upon his first arrest, her parents said, their daughter's killer would have been found three years earlier. In 2006 the New Mexico state legislature passed "Katie's Law," which requires law enforcement officials to take DNA samples from most felony arrests. Several other states have followed suit.

In a 2010 interview with John Walsh, the host of the TV show *America's Most Wanted*, President Barack Obama agreed that there should be a national database of DNA profiles of every person arrested, whether convicted or not. "We have eighteen states who are taking DNA upon arrest," Walsh said. "It's no different than fingerprinting or

X and Y Markers

n most mammals, the sex of an offspring is determined by the X and Y chromosomes. Females have two X chromosomes—one inherited from each parent. Males have one X chromosome, inherited from the mother, and one Y chromosome, inherited from the father. Scientists have identified more than two hundred STR loci on the Y chromosome; between nine and eleven of these markers may be used in forensic science. These markers are especially useful at crime scenes where there is a mixture of evidence from a male and female, or from several males. Because the Y chromosome is passed directly from a father to his sons, it can also be used to trace family relationships among males, such as in paternity testing.

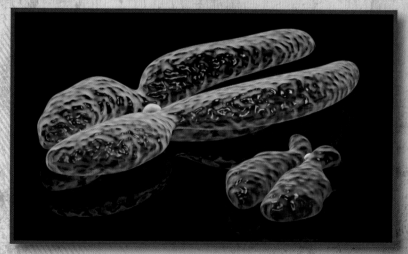

This 3D illustration shows an X chromosome (green) and a Y chromosome (blue).

a booking photo." President Obama believed that a national registry would help in the finding and conviction of those previously registered within the database.[7]

Several countries do have national DNA databases of everyone who has been arrested for a crime, but many people believe that such databases violate an individual's right to privacy. They worry that it may unjustly target minorities.

Michael Seringhaus, a student at Yale Law School, wrote an editorial in the *New York Times* proposing that we keep every American's DNA profile on record. "A universal record would be a strong deterrent to first-time offenders," he wrote. "After all, any DNA sample left behind would be a smoking gun for the police—and would enable police to more quickly apprehend repeat criminals. It would also help prevent wrongful convictions. . . . Since every American would have a stake in keeping the data private and ensuring that only the limited content vital to law enforcement was recorded, there would be far less likelihood of government misuse than in the case of a more selective database."[8]

The O. J. Simpson Trial

Even the most compelling DNA and blood evidence can be called into question if jurors can be convinced that investigators mishandled forensic evidence. This is exactly what happened during one of the most sensational and famous cases of the twentieth

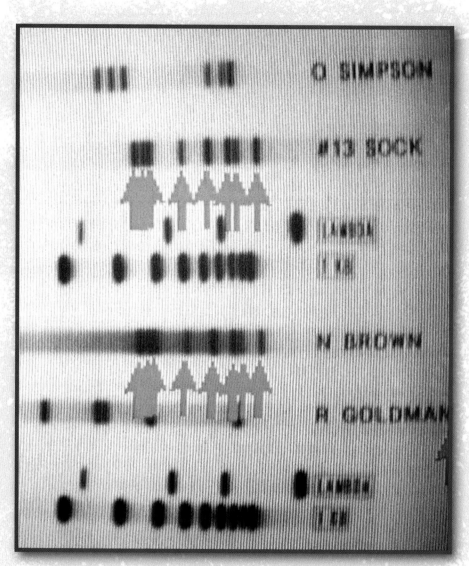

A DNA X-ray film presented at the O. J. Simpson trial showed that blood on a pair of socks found in Simpson's bedroom matched DNA belonging to Nicole Brown Simpson.

century: the murder trial of Orenthal James (O. J.) Simpson, a famous former football star.

On June 12, 1994, the bodies of Simpson's ex-wife, Nicole Brown Simpson, and her friend Ronald Goldman were found just outside Nicole Simpson's Los Angeles apartment. Both had been brutally stabbed to death.

The Simpsons' seventeen-year relationship had been a rocky one, ending in divorce in 1993. O. J. Simpson was the prime suspect, and the case against him seemed airtight. A trail of bloody shoe prints at the murder scene were made by the same size and make of shoes owned by Mr. Simpson and contained DNA that matched his. A bloodstained left-handed glove found on Nicole Brown Simpson's property contained Mr. Simpson's DNA, as well as that of both victims. When the police questioned Mr. Simpson, they discovered a cut on his left hand. DNA from hair samples found on Mr. Goldman's body after the murder also matched Mr. Simpson's DNA. Blood in Mr. Simpson's Ford Bronco contained DNA from both Ms. Simpson and Mr. Goldman. A pair of bloodstained socks found in Mr. Simpson's bedroom contained Mrs. Simpson's DNA.

O. J. Simpson's trial lasted nine months and received widespread media coverage. Mr. Simpson's defense team included Robert Kardashian and F. Lee Bailey, the lawyer who had successfully defended Sam Sheppard in his second murder trial. The defense lawyers claimed that the police officers were racist and cast doubt upon the methods and competence of the laboratories that had carried out the DNA analysis. Despite the overwhelming evidence that Mr. Simpson had murdered his ex-wife and her friend, the jurors were not convinced that the blood samples had been handled appropriately. They found O. J. Simpson not guilty on both charges.

Even though Mr. Simpson was found not guilty in a criminal court, Ron Goldman's family brought a civil case against him. There is a lower threshold for proof of liability in a civil trial (in a civil court, defendants are found liable, rather than guilty). The lawyers did not have to prove that Simpson was guilty beyond a reasonable doubt—only that most of the evidence linked him to the murders. In this case, the jurors found Mr. Simpson liable of the murders and ordered him to pay $8.5 million in damages to the Goldman family.

In 2006, O. J. Simpson was planning on writing a book called *If I Did It*. It would have been his view, a hypothetical account, of the murders. The publishing deal fell through and the rights of the book were awarded to Ronald Goldman's family. They renamed it *If I Did It: Confessions of the Killer* and published it in 2007. The following year, Simpson was convicted on twelve counts of armed robbery. He was found guilty of robbing sports memorabilia from dealers at gunpoint. In 2016, his trial came back into the spotlight through the FX miniseries *American Crime Story: The People v. O. J. Simpson*.[9]

GUILTY UNTIL PROVEN INNOCENT

magine that a crime has been committed. A suspect has been apprehended. You have an eyewitness who identifies the suspect from a police lineup and after hours of interrogation, the suspect finally confesses. Case closed, right? Wrong.

Not What You Think You Saw

Studies have shown that eyewitness evidence is not always reliable. Memory is a tricky thing. Elizabeth Loftus, a memory expert who has testified in more than 250 hearings and trials, did an experiment in which she showed subjects six photos while they listened to a crime story. One out of the six photos showed the culprit; the other five were of innocent characters. Three days later, she showed the subjects a photo of one of the innocent characters, along with photos of three new people. She asked them to pick the criminal from these four photos. Twenty-four percent of the subjects said that the criminal was not among the photos (the correct response). Sixteen percent picked one of the new characters. Sixty percent picked the most familiar face—the innocent character whose photo they'd seen both times.[1]

Mistaken eyewitness testimony can be triggered by subtle cues from police officers or detectives, a gap in memory, or a desire to make an identification at all costs. Loftus and other researchers have also found that if the perpetrator is not in the initial lineup, witnesses tend to pick somebody who resembles the criminal. They just assume that the real perpetrator is in the lineup, and it's their job to recognize him.

Faulty eyewitness testimony is the single greatest cause of wrongful convictions nationwide, according to the Innocence Project. It plays a role in more than 75 percent of convictions overturned by DNA testing. Eyewitness testimony can be a valuable tool in the criminal justice system, but as with all evidence, it needs to be handled with care.

Researcher Elizabeth Loftus found that people assume the perpetrator is in a lineup, even if he or she isn't, which often leads to wrongful convictions.

False Confessions

So the eyewitness was wrong. But the suspect admitted he did it. You may be surprised to learn that admitting you're guilty doesn't always mean you're actually guilty. According to the Innocence Project, defendants made incriminating statements,

Protections Against Identifying the Wrong Suspect

The Innocence Project has several suggestions that would make eyewitness testimony more reliable:

- The person carrying out the photo or live lineup should not know who the real suspect is.

- "Fillers," or the nonsuspects in the lineup, should resemble the eyewitness's description of the criminal; one person shouldn't stand out too much from the others. Eyewitnesses should not view more than one lineup with the same suspect.

- The eyewitness should be told that the perpetrator might not be in the lineup.

- Immediately after the viewing the lineup, the eyewitness should give a statement about his or her confidence in the identification.

- Members in the lineup should be presented one at a time rather than all at once, if possible. Research has shown that this decreases the rate at which innocent people are picked out of a lineup.

confessed, or pled guilty in about 25 percent of the cases where DNA evidence later proved their innocence. Why would anyone confess to a crime they didn't commit?

Confessions from children and teenagers, as well as those with mental disabilities, are often unreliable. Aggressive investigators easily influence them. Among the other reasons innocent people confess to crimes they didn't commit are harsh interrogation tactics, fear of violence and torture, and mental impairment due to alcohol or drug use.

The following case illustrates how faulty eyewitness testimony and a false confession turned the lives of two innocent young men upside down.

The Murder Case Against Travis Hayes and Ryan Matthews

In April 1997, a masked man entered a convenience store in Bridge City, Louisiana, and shot the owner, Tommy Vanhoose, to death after he refused to hand over the money. One witness was in her car at the time and saw the masked man briefly pull up his ski mask in the parking lot. He fired shots in her direction as he ran and dove through the open passenger window of a large car.

Two other witnesses said that the man had shed his mask, gloves, and shirt as he fled the scene. They confirmed that he was shooting his gun, and the driver of the car had seen the gunman's face in his rearview mirror.

When a masked man killed a Louisiana convenience store owner, no one could positively identify the culprit. Yet two young friends who were at the wrong place at the wrong time were pulled over by the police and arrested.

Several hours later, 11 miles (18 kilometers) from the crime, two seventeen-year-old boys in a primer-gray 1981 Pontiac Grande Prix were pulled over by the police. Travis Hayes, the driver, and his friend, Ryan Matthews, were just driving around while listening to hip-hop music on the car stereo.

The friends thought little of it at first; they had seen plenty of young black men pulled over by the police for seemingly no reason. But their car was similar to the description of the getaway car, and that made them prime suspects in Vanhoose's murder.

Hayes initially told police that he and Matthews had not been in the area where the murder had occurred. But after six hours of questioning, he changed his story. Hayes, who was mentally disabled, told investigators that he had driven with Matthews to the store and watched as his friend went inside. Fifteen minutes later, he said, he heard shots and saw Matthews run out. Matthews, on the other hand, maintained his innocence.

Two years later, Ryan Matthews went on trial for the murder of Tommy Vanhoose. The defense presented evidence that the DNA from the inside of the ski mask did not match that of Matthews or Hayes. Witnesses said that the masked gunman had dived through the open car window, but the passenger window of the Grand Prix had been stuck closed for a long time. Other witnesses had described the perpetrator as short. Matthews was 6 feet (183 cm) tall.

The jury was swayed by eyewitnesses who testified that Matthews was the man they had seen running out of the store. Hayes's confession seemed to confirm his guilt. Matthews was convicted of first-degree murder and sentenced to death. Hayes was convicted of second-degree murder and sentenced to life in prison without parole.

Matthews and Hayes, serving time in Louisiana's Angola prison farm, were desperate to prove their innocence. William Sothern and Clive Stafford Smith, attorneys with the Louisiana Crisis Assistance Center, thought that Matthews had not been given a fair trial. They appealed his case.

Sothern heard that a man in prison for an unrelated murder had been bragging to other prisoners about killing Tommy Vanhoose. The man, Rondell Love, had slashed the throat of a young woman named Chandra Conley just eight months after Vanhoose's murder. Sothern found that there was a DNA profile on file for Love. He compared Love's DNA profile with the DNA that had been found around the mouth of the ski mask. They were an exact match.

A case worker for the Innocence Project stands next to folders containing cases of prisoners who have asked for help in proving their innocence.

Ryan Matthews was granted a new trial. Based in part on the DNA evidence, the jury found him innocent of the charges. He was released from prison in 2004. He had become the fourteenth death row inmate in the United States to be proven innocent with DNA testing.

Even though Matthews had been declared innocent, Hayes remained in prison for two more years before attorneys at the Innocence Project managed to win his release. Together, the two men had served thirteen years in prison for a crime they did not commit.

The Innocence Project continues to work hard to give wrongfully convicted prisoners their lives back. So far, 349 people who were previously convicted have been found innocent through DNA testing, including 20 people who served time on death row.[2]

CHAPTER 6

SOLVING ONE OF HISTORY'S MYSTERIES

People are still fascinated by history's most famous crimes and unsolved mysteries, and studios still release TV shows and movies about them. The story of Anastasia Romanov, the Russian princess who many believed escaped the tragic fate that befell her family during the Russian Revolution in the early twentieth century, has been told and retold in countless books, documentaries, films, and even an animated musical and Broadway play. Nearly a century after the events took place, DNA evidence finally brought closure to the cold case that became a legendary tale.

The Romanovs

On July 17, 1918, Tsar Nicholas II of the House of Romanov; his wife, Alexandra; their

The Romanovs were the last royal family of Russia. Olga and Tatiana stand in the back. Seated from left to right are Maria, Queen Alexandra, Tsar Nicholas II, and Anastasia. Alexei sits in the front on the floor.

five children, Olga, Maria, Tatiana, Anastasia, and Alexei; servants; and the family doctor were led to the cellar of a house in Ekaterinburg, Siberia, where they were held captive. The Romanov family had ruled Russia from 1613 until the Bolsheviks (later known as Communists) took power in 1917.

Once the family and staff were assembled in the cellar, their captor, Yakov Yurovsky, called in a firing squad. Yurovsky shot the tsar, and the firing squad shot the rest. The headline of the local newspaper read, "Execution of Nicholas, the Bloody Crowned Murderer—Shot Without Bourgeois Formalities but in Accordance With Our New Democratic Principles."[1]

Six months later, a Russian investigator found several pieces of evidence from the supposed grave site, but no skeletons. The location of the remains of the Romanovs was a mystery until 1989, when two amateur Russian historians announced that they had located the grave. In 1991 the Russian government authorized an official forensic investigation of the grave. Investigators recovered one thousand bone fragments that were assembled into five female and four male skeletons.

Russian forensic experts used computer software to superimpose the skulls with pictures of the Romanovs and their staff, compared the teeth with dental records, and measured the bones to determine the ages and sexes of the remains. They readily identified Nicholas II and his wife.

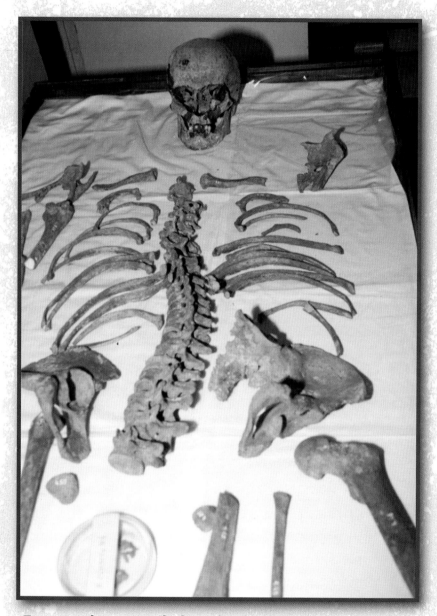

Experts determined that the bones of a fairly short middle-aged man showing signs of wear and tear due to years of horseback riding (a favorite activity of the tsar) were those of Nicholas II.

The scientists identified the other four adult skeletons as the remains of the royal physician, the family cook, Nicholas's personal attendant (all male), and the maid.

Forensic anthropologists determined that the remaining three skeletons probably belonged to the three oldest daughters. There was some dispute as to whether one of the skeletons identified actually belonged to the youngest daughter, Anastasia, or her sister Maria.

At any rate, two skeletons were missing: that of either Anastasia or Maria, and that of thirteen-year-old Alexei, the heir to the throne. The missing skeletons fueled mass speculation that Alexei and one of the two younger daughters had somehow escaped execution and were living secret lives elsewhere.

To confirm the bone studies, government authorities asked Russian biologist Pavel Ivanov to carry out DNA testing on the bones. Ivanov arranged to conduct the tests in collaboration with Peter Gill at the British Forensic Science Service. He flew from Moscow to London with pieces of the leg bones of each of the nine skeletons in his carry-on bag.

The scientists had their work cut out for them since there was very little DNA left to analyze. First, they determined the sex of each skeleton by analyzing a gene on the X chromosome that is six base pairs longer than the similar gene on the Y chromosome. They used the PCR technique to

Analyzing Mitochondrial DNA

Although most DNA resides within the nucleus of the cell, there is another important place to find DNA in the cell—the mitochondria. Mitochondria are tiny structures that turn oxygen and nutrients into energy to power the cell. The number of mitochondria in each cell varies according to its energy needs; liver cells, for example, contain between one thousand and two thousand of these little powerhouses.

Each mitochondrion carries two to ten copies of DNA to help carry out its functions. Regular DNA comes from both parents, but mtDNA comes just from the mother. Although mitochondrial DNA contains just 16,569 base pairs, it can be very useful in some forensic cases. Because mtDNA is inherited through the mother's line, scientists can help solve a cold case by analyzing and comparing the mtDNA profile of unidentified remains with any maternal relative. The FBI started using mtDNA analysis to solve cold cases in 1996.

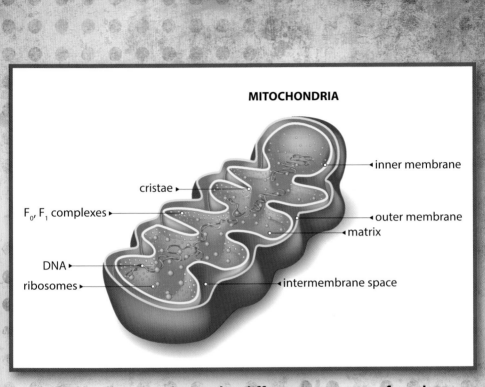

MITOCHONDRIA

inner membrane

cristae

F_0, F_1 complexes

outer membrane

matrix

DNA

ribosomes

intermembrane space

This diagram shows the different structures found in a cell's mitochondria. The DNA (shown as pink ribbons) comes from the maternal side of the family and proves useful in discovering the identity of unknown remains.

amplify STR sequences to reveal a mother, a father, and their three daughters. They still had to prove that the bones were indeed those of the Romanov family. For that they turned to mitochondrial DNA.

Mitochondrial DNA (mtDNA) is inherited only from the mother. In order to create a mtDNA profile for each of the nine skeletons, the scientists needed to find living relatives of the Romanovs to compare the DNA profiles to. Fortunately, Prince Philip, Duke of Edinburgh, was Alexandra's great-nephew. Prince Philip agreed to help, and he sent Gill and Ivanov a test tube of his blood. The match was perfect: the mother, three daughters, and Prince Philip all shared the same mtDNA sequences.

Finding a reference sample for Nicholas proved more difficult. The tsar's nephew, Tikhon Kulikovsky, refused to cooperate. The scientists pored over Nicholas's family tree to find other relatives with the same maternal bloodline. They found two distant relatives, Xenia Sfiris and the Duke of Fife, who agreed to send blood samples.

The mtDNA of Xenia Sfiris and the Duke of Fife matched exactly. But when the scientists compared that DNA with the sample they thought belonged to the tsar, they found one mismatch out of 781 base pairs. Where Sfiris and the Duke of Fife had a thymine, Nicholas had a cytosine. Puzzled, the scientists ran the test again. This time, some of the genes matched those of Sfiris and the duke; others repeated the same mismatching cytosine. The scientists concluded that Nicholas had two forms of mitochondrial DNA, a condition known as heteroplasmy. They published their results, saying that there was a 98.5 percent chance that these remains had belonged to Nicholas II.

Doubt still surrounded the identity of the bones presumed to be those of Nicholas II. In 1994 the scientists were given permission to analyze the DNA from the body of Nicholas's brother, Georgij, who had died in 1899. They analyzed the DNA and found that Georgij had the same rare forms of two mitochondrial DNA. The mystery of five members of the Romanov family was finally laid to rest. The two missing children, Alexi and Anastasia, were still unaccounted for.

The Grand Duchess, Anastasia

Years after the execution, many women claimed to be the lost daughter, Anastasia. There was one, called Anna, who stood out from the rest. She claimed that she was rescued by a soldier and smuggled into Germany. She came to Berlin to seek help from her maternal aunt, Princess Irene of Prussia. When the two met, Princess Irene did not recognize her. "I saw immediately that she could not be one of my nieces," Irene wrote. "Even though I had not seen them for nine years, the fundamental facial characteristics could not have altered to that degree, in particular the position of the eyes, the ears, and so forth."[2]

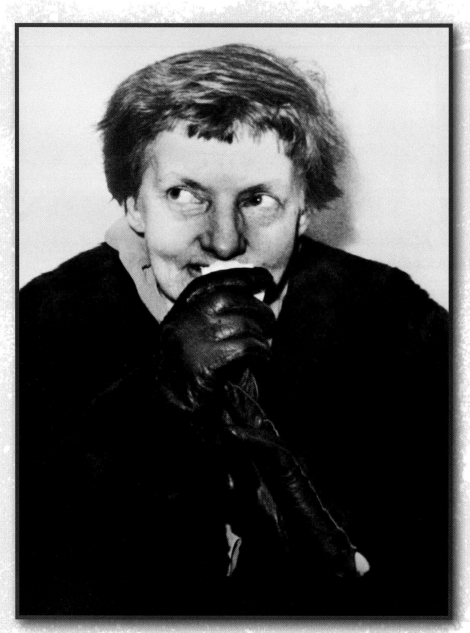

Anna Anderson, pictured here in 1955, claimed to be the Grand Duchess Anastasia, the youngest daughter of Tsar Nicholas II, until her dying day. Later DNA tests proved that Anderson was not a Romanov.

In 1927, a German woman said that Anna was actually Franziska Schanzkowska. She revealed that Franziska, a Polish factory worker whose family were peasants, had been a lodger in her mother's home until her abrupt disappearance in 1920. Even so, Anna had many supporters who believed her story, including the son of the Romanov family doctor. Anna eventually moved to Charlottesville, Virginia, where she went by the name Anna Anderson. She held fast to her story until her death in 1984.

After the 1991 finding that the bones of Alexei and one of the sisters were missing from the grave site, there was a renewed interest in Anderson's identity. Although she was cremated, a hospital in Charlottesville still had some tissue samples that had been removed following an operation. After a yearlong battle over who had the rights to test the tissue sample, it went to Peter Gill. In 1994, Gill confirmed that Anna Anderson was by no means related to the Romanov family.

In 2007, a group of amateur archaeologists discovered a second grave just 230 feet (70 meters) from the original Romanov burial site. The grave held charred bone fragments and teeth of an adolescent boy and of a girl who had been somewhat older. The Russian government asked an international team of scientists to carry out DNA testing on the bones. They reconstructed the entire mitochondrial gene sequences of the bones, conducted STR analysis on the nuclear DNA, and analyzed Y-chromosome markers of the male bones. The results were clear: these were the bones of the missing children, Alexei and one of his sisters.

After ninety years, cutting-edge DNA forensics had finally solved one of the most enduring mysteries of the twentieth century.

CHAPTER 7

KILLING FOR PROFIT

According to the University of Florida's International Veterinary Forensic Sciences Association (IVFSA), "Wildlife crime is a billion-dollar threat that spans across countries and continents. Between poaching, illegal trade and regulation issues, there are many immediate issues facing some of the world's most endangered species."[1] African elephants, the largest animals on land, are among the most well-known species facing extinction at the hands of poachers.

Financing Terror

Samuel K. Wasser, a conservation biologist at the University of Washington, discovered two elephant skulls lying side by side in a game reserve in Tanzania, a country in central East Africa. One skull had belonged to a baby elephant and the other was its mother.

The dental pattern of the two skulls was almost identical with the only difference being the size of the teeth. Clearly, the adult and baby elephants had been related.

He understood immediately what had happened; Poachers had killed the baby elephant in order to draw the grieving mother elephant close enough to kill her and cut off her enormous ivory tusks to sell later.[2]

Horrific scenarios like this have been played out thousands of times in past decades across much of Africa. In 1979, there were an estimated 1.3 million African elephants; today, only about 415,000 remain.[3,4] Much of the decline of African elephants is due to rampant poaching.

In 1989, the Convention on International Trade in Endangered Species (CITES, a United Nations organization) banned international trade in ivory. Demand for ivory dried up, and for a time it seemed

An African elephant family roams the grasslands in Botswana. Unfortunately, these majestic creatures are poached for their beautiful ivory tusks.

as though elephants might be safe from poachers.

In the 1990s, three African countries—Botswana, Namibia, and Zimbabwe—persuaded CITES to place elephants on a less endangered status and to allow them to sell their stockpiled ivory abroad. Around the same time, people in some Asian countries were becoming more prosperous. Beautiful objects carved from ivory were a status symbol. The demand for ivory soared. Powerful and well-armed gangs of poachers and ivory traders began killing elephants by the thousands. They bribed corrupt customs officials and hid ivory in shipment containers that were shuttled between as many as half a dozen countries between Africa and Asia in order to avoid detection.

Tracking the Ivory

Until recently it was nearly impossible to track down poachers. If law enforcement agents seized an illegal shipment of ivory, they had no way of telling where it had come from. Dealers could claim that their ivory came from domesticated Asian elephants, which is legal. But thanks to DNA profiling, law enforcement officials have a new tool to help them track down

Once poachers get their hands on the tusks, the contraband are then carved into beautiful figurines and other objects and sold to the rich.

the origin of the ivory. Over a decade, with the help of many scientists and game wardens, Wasser collected hundreds of elephant dung samples from all across sub-Saharan Africa. Each sample, containing DNA from millions of cells shed from the

Busted with Illegal Ivory

When US Fish and Wildlife Service special agents searched Moun Chau's donut shop in Claremont, California, in 2007, they found more than glazed donuts and apple fritters. Following an undercover operation, they seized dozens of ivory items worth thousands of dollars. Chau had purchased the ivory, advertised for sale on eBay, from a Thai businessman named Samart Chokchoyma. The businessman shipped the goods to Chau in packages marked as toys.

Scientists at the US Fish and Wildlife Service Forensics Laboratory in Ashland, Oregon, used DNA testing to confirm that the ivory had come from African elephants. In January 2010, US authorities arrested Chau. Chokchoyma was arrested by Thai police. Both men were charged with several crimes, including violating the US Endangered Species Act. Officials don't believe that Chokchoyma was the ringleader of the ivory smuggling gang, which probably includes members from several countries. But it is a start.

elephant's intestine, was shipped back to Wasser's lab at the University of Washington. He analyzed sixteen separate short tandem repeats (STRs) of DNA to create a reference profile for the elephant genome. Armed with the DNA profiles of dung samples from known geographic areas, and knowing that the genetic makeup of elephants living close to each other is more similar than elephants living far apart, Wasser was able to create a genetic map of the animals.

In 2006, authorities seized nearly 24,251 pounds (11,000 kg or 11 metric tons) of elephant ivory from Taiwan, Hong Kong, and Japan. Officials from Taiwan and Hong Kong sent samples of the seized ivory to Wasser's lab in Washington. These tusks had come from elephants in Tanzania and northern Mozambique. At a CITES meeting in March 2010, both Zambia and Tanzania asked to again be allowed to sell ivory that had been stockpiled, arguing that they had elephant poaching and the illegal ivory trade well under control. The delegates at the meeting turned both countries down, based in part on the DNA evidence. Conservation experts say that even legal trade in elephant tusks just adds to the desire for more ivory, encouraging even more poaching and illegal trade.

In 2016, Kenya burned their largest stockpile of illegal ivory. In Nairobi National Park, tusks from over six thousand slaughtered elephants were set alight. Kenya's president, Uhuru Kenyatta, stated

Illegal stockpiles of elephant tusks, ivory figurines, and rhinoceros horns burn in Nairobi National Park on April 30, 2016, to discourage poachers and demonstrate the need for a total ban on the trafficking of ivory.

that the burning was to convey the message that "ivory is worthless unless it is on our elephants," and discourage poachers from killing more elephants and rhinos.[5] Although there is still much work to do, there are charities and campaigns set up to stop the illegal ivory trade. There are also wildlife sanctuaries in which the animals roam freely without fear of being killed for profit.

Career Information

Are you naturally curious? Do you enjoy solving mysteries? Do you find anatomy and physiology fascinating? Then forensic science may be the right career path for you. A bachelor's degree in chemistry, biology, or physics is required. In addition to scientific and technical knowledge, you also need to know how to communicate clearly. Forensic scientists who testify in court need good speaking skills, so join a debate team or take a course in public speaking.

There are several career specialties available to people interested in DNA and blood forensics. Criminalists analyze, identify, and interpret physical evidence. To become a certified criminalist, you must have a bachelor's degree in the physical or natural sciences.

If you are interested in DNA testing, you should take courses in genetics, molecular biology, statistics, and biochemistry. You also need two years of experience working in a forensics laboratory, and you must pass a certification examination. Criminalists work in forensic laboratories in police departments, sheriff's offices, district attorney's offices, regional and state agencies, medical examiners and coroner's offices, private companies, or colleges and universities. They may also work for federal agencies, such as the Federal Bureau of Investigation, the Central Intelligence Agency, the military, or the US Fish and Wildlife Service.

Crime scene investigators must have a bachelor's degree, either in a physical or a natural science, or in criminal justice. They assess, document, and gather evidence at crime scenes; view autopsies; meet with law enforcement officials; prepare detailed crime scene reports; and testify in court. Experts in bloodstain pattern analysis have a good working knowledge of math, physics, biology, and chemistry. They may work for many of the same agencies that employ criminalists, but the difference is that they do more fieldwork. Income and job opportunities vary greatly depending on your degree, your specialty, and where you work. According to the Occupational Outlook Handbook by the US Bureau of Labor Statistics, the median pay for a forensic science technician in 2015 was $56,750. And the employment opportunities for forensic science technicians is expected to increase by 27 percent until 2024.[1] The work can be challenging and emotionally draining

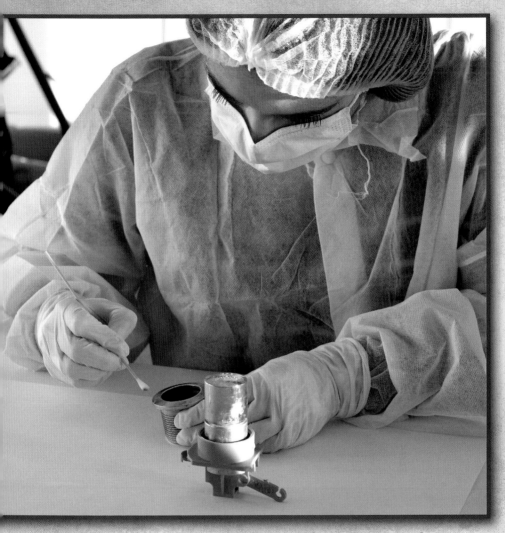

A lab technician tests the DNA of a fingerprint for an investigation. DNA analysis is just one of the many areas of expertise in forensic science.

at times as you piece together the last moments of a person's life. However, playing an essential part in bringing closure to a grieving family and bringing the perpetrator to justice makes a career in forensic science a rewarding one.

CHAPTER 1. Evidence of Blood

1. Fred McGunagle, "Sam Sheppard," *True Crime Library: Criminal Minds and Methods*, n.d., http://www.trutv.com/library/crime/notorious_murders/famous/sheppard/index_1.html.

2. Ibid.

3. Cynthia L. Cooper and Sam Reese Sheppard, *Mockery of Justice: The True Story of the Sheppard Murder Case* (Boston, Mass.: Northeastern University Press, 1995), p. 112.

CHAPTER 2. Blood or Dye?

1. Paul Uhlenhuth, "Concerning My New Forensic Method to Identify Human Blood," *Sourcebook in Forensic Serology, Immunology, and Biochemistry. Unit IX: Translations of Selected Contributions to the Original Literature of Medicolegal Examinations of Blood and Body Fluids* (National Institute of Justice, Research Foundation of the City University of New York, 1983), p. 177.

2. Sir Arthur Conan Doyle, "A Study in Scarlet," *Sherlock Holmes: The Complete Novels and Stories, Volume 1* (New York, N.Y.: Bantam Dell/Random House, 2003), pp. 7–8.

3. Christine L. Huber, "The Sherlock Holmes Blood Test: The Solution to a Century-old Mystery," *Sherlock Holmes by Gas-Lamp: Highlights from the First Four Decades of the Baker Street Journal*

(New York, N.Y.: Fordham University Press, 1989), pp. 95–101.

CHAPTER 3. Forensic Serology

1. University of Colorado at Boulder, "New Hand Bacteria Study Holds Promise for Forensics Identification," *ScienceDaily*, March 16, 2010, http://www.sciencedaily.com/releases/2010/03/100315161718.htm.

2. "Blood Spatters Reveal a Suspect's Age Through New Technique," *Phys.org*, March 21, 2017, https://phys.org/news/2017-03-blood-spatters-reveal-age-technique.html.

3. Colin Evans, *The Casebook of Forensic Detection: How Science Solved 100 of the World's Most Baffling Crimes* (New York, N.Y.: John Wiley & Sons, 1996), p. 210.

CHAPTER 4. DNA Profiling

1. Henry C. Lee, PhD, and Frank Tirnady, *Blood Evidence: How DNA Is Revolutionizing the Way We Solve Crimes* (Cambridge, Mass.: Perseus Publishing, 2003), p. 6.

2. Andrew Lyons, "Terror on Telford Lane. Part IV: An Already Tense Situation Escalates," *Daytona Beach News–Journal*, April 9, 2006, http://www.news-journalonline.com/special/deltonadeaths/frtHEAD02040906.htm.

3. Ibid.

4. Ibid.

5. Patricio G. Balona, "DNA Testimony Strongest Yet in Deltona Murder Trial," *Daytona Beach News–*

Journal, July 19, 2006, http:// www.news-journal online.com/special/deltonadeaths/frtHEAD0207 1906.htm.

6. Patricio G. Balona, "Inmate: 'Disrespect' Spurred Victorino to Kill," *Daytona Beach News–Journal*, November 8, 2005, http://www.news-journalonline .com/special/deltonadeaths/03AreaWEST 01110805.htm.

7. White House Blog, "President Obama on 'America's Most Wanted,'" *Whitehouse.gov*, March 6, 2010, http://www.whitehouse.gov/blog/2010/03/05/ president-obama-americas-most-wanted.

8. Michael Seringhaus, "To Stop Crime, Share Your Genes," *New York Times*, March 15, 2010, p. A21.

9. "O. J. Simpson Biography," *Biography.com*, September 9, 2016, http://www.biography.com/ people/oj-simpson-9484729

CHAPTER 5. Guilty Until Proven Innocent

1. William Saletan, "Leading the Witness: Contaminated Memories and Criminal Justice," *Slate .com*, May 26, 2010, http://www.slate.com/id/225 1882/pagenum/2.

2. Innocence Project, "DNA Exonerations in the United States," *Innocence Project*, n.d., https:// www.innocenceproject.org/dna-exonerations-in-the -united-states/.

CHAPTER 6. Solving One of History's Mysteries

1. Robert K. Massie, *The Romanovs: The Final Chapter* (New York, N.Y.: Random House, 1995), pp. 23–24.

2. Ibid., p. 167.

CHAPTER 7. Killing for Profit

1. "Overview: Wildlife Forensic Sciences and Conservation," *University of Florida*, April 21, 2017, https://wildlife.forensics.med.ufl.edu/.
2. Samuel K. Wasser, Bill Clark, and Cathy Laurie, "The Ivory Trail," *Scientific American*, July 2009, p. 76.
3. "Key Milestones in Elephant Conservation," *Great Elephant Census*, n.d., http://www.greatelephant census.com/background-on-conservation/.
4. "African Elephants," *WWF Global*, n.d., http://wwf .panda.org/what_we_do/endangered_species/ elephants/african_elephants/.
5. Rachel Nuwer, "Kenya Sets Ablaze 105 Tons of Ivory," *National Geographic*, April 30, 2016, http://news.nationalgeographic.com/2016/ 04/160430-kenya-record-breaking-ivory-burn/.

CAREER INFORMATION

1. Bureau of Labor Statistics, US Department of Labor, *Occupational Outlook Handbook, 2016–17 Edition*, Forensic Science Technicians, May 2015, https:// www.bls.gov/ooh/life-physical-and-social-science/ forensic-science-technicians.htm.

adenine One of the four bases in a DNA molecule; adenine (A) always pairs with thymine (T).

anthropologist A scientist who identifies and examines human skeletal remains.

antibody A protein produced in response to and that neutralizes a specific antigen.

antigen A molecule that induces an immune response in the body.

base pair Two complementary nucleotide bases held together by a hydrogen bond in the DNA molecule; e.g., adenine–thymine, guanine–cytosine.

bloodstain pattern analysis The science of studying the patterns left by blood on various surfaces in order to determine the events that led to their creation. The patterns are also known as blood spatter.

CODIS Combined DNA Index System, the national DNA database that contains genetic profiles from convicted felons as well as profiles obtained from crime scene evidence.

cold case An old unsolved criminal case.

coroner A public official whose chief duty is to discover the cause of death, especially one that might not be due to natural causes.

cytosine One of the four bases in a DNA molecule; cytosine (C) always pairs with guanine (G).

DNA profiling The process of using DNA characteristics to identify an individual.

forensic science The field of science that uses principles of biology, physics, and chemistry to analyze evidence from crimes scenes.

guanine One of the four bases in a DNA molecule; guanine (G) always pairs with cytosine (C).

hemoglobin A red blood cell protein responsible for transporting oxygen in the bloodstream.

locus (plural loci) The specific location of a gene or coding sequence on a chromosome.

medical examiner Someone appointed by the city, who is trained in the medical field, and can perform autopsies to investigate crimes.

nucleotide One of the building blocks of DNA.

secretor An individual who carries his or her blood group antigens in body fluids, including saliva and sweat.

serology The study of blood and other bodily fluids.

serum The clear yellowish liquid obtained after separating whole blood into its solid and liquid components after it has been allowed to clot.

thymine One of the four bases in a DNA molecule; thymine (T) always pair with adenine (A).

trajectory The path of a projectile.

FURTHER READING

Books

Gardner, Robert, and Joshua Conklin. *Experiments for Future Forensic Scientists.* New York, NY: Enslow Publishing, 2017.

Heos, Bridget. *Blood, Bullets, and Bones: The Story of Forensic Science from Sherlock Holmes to DNA.* New York, NY: Balzer & Bray, 2016.

Innes, Brian. *Forensic Science.* Broomall, PA: Mason Crest, 2016.

Mooney, Carla. *Genetics: Breaking the Code of Your DNA.* Nomad Press: White River Junction, VT, 2014.

Rauf, Don, and Judith Williams. *Forensic Science Specialists.* New York, NY: Enslow Publishing, 2015.

Sutinis, Beth. *Crime Scene Techs!* Broomall, PA: Mason Crest, 2015.

Websites

American Academy of Forensic Sciences
www.aafs.org/
Find more information about what forensic scientists do, the different types of forensic scientists, and programs offered at colleges and universities.

BioNinja, DNA Profiling
ib.bioninja.com.au/standard-level/topic-3-
genetics/35-genetic-modification-and/
dna-profiling.html
Learn more about DNA profiling and practice with a simple activity.

Crime Scene Investigator Network
www.crime-scene-investigator.net
Read articles on forensic science subjects, explore links to courses, and browse resources on how to become a crime scene investigator.